"In a world where change is constant and certainty is rare, traditional goal-setting often falls short. This book serves as a guide for leaders, entrepreneurs, and visionaries ready to navigate uncharted territory."

Achieving The Unknown

© 2025 16042899 Canada Inc.

All rights reserved. No part of this book may be reproduced, distributed, or transmitted in any form or by any means, including photocopying, recording, or other electronic or mechanical methods, without the prior written permission of the publisher, except in the case of brief quotations embodied in critical reviews, articles, or educational use.

This book is a work of nonfiction. While drawn from the author's professional and personal experience, it is intended for informational purposes only. The author and publisher make no representations or warranties with respect to the accuracy or completeness of the contents. They specifically disclaim any liability for damages resulting from the use of the information contained herein.

First Edition, 2025

Cover and interior design by Ramit Soni

Leading Into The Unknown

Every great venture begins with something unknown – a vision not yet clear, a goal not yet defined, a future not yet shaped. For founders, executives, and professionals, stepping into the unknown is both daunting and exhilarating. In business and life, we are often trained to set concrete goals and make linear plans. Yet what do we do when the goal itself is murky or the path uncharted? How do we achieve something we can't even fully articulate yet?

This book presents a contemplative framework for achieving the unknown. It is a **reflective** and **instructional** journey designed for high-level leaders who are accustomed to driving forward, but who sense that a different, more mindful approach is needed when navigating uncertainty. The insights and methods here are drawn from the author's personal notes and experiences, infused with a unique perspective on **mindful leadership, self-trust, and purpose**. While it is informed by deep personal wisdom (inspired in part by the author's own profile in an introspective system), it is presented here simply as a human perspective – no jargon or esoteric systems required.

In these pages, you will discover:

- How to **believe in the existence of an as-yet unseen solution or outcome**, and why that mindset is the foundation for any great achievement.
- Why you must **attach to the journey and detach from the outcome**, investing fully in the process while releasing obsessive concern over results.
- The practice of **observing, feeling, and allowing** your experiences instead of constantly controlling them – and how this openness leads to genuine discovery.
- The power of **pausing** – taking intentional breaks to reflect and refresh – and how increasing your pauses can unlock creativity and clarity.
- How to notice the subtle **"flashes of interest"** that spark your curiosity, and to explore these sparks as clues toward the unknown.

- A **contemplative loop** of pivoting and persevering: a cycle where you periodically adjust your direction (pivot) and persist through challenges (persevere), which ultimately leads to progress.
- Frameworks for **filtering and contemplating ideas** before leaping into action, ensuring that what you pursue has meaning and resonance.
- Why **transforming control into authority** is the key to mindful leadership – letting go of micromanaging and instead stepping into genuine, earned influence.
- The concept of a **"liberating purpose"** – a purpose that not only drives you but also frees you, and how perseverance on this path leads to profound fulfillment.

The tone of this book is part gentle reflection and part practical guidance. You will find poetic insights alongside actionable advice. It is not a rigid formula – it's a flexible framework. Think of it as a trusted companion on your journey: offering structure and wisdom while leaving plenty of space for your own insights and interpretation.

Whether you are a CEO steering an organization through ambiguity, a startup founder seeking a viable vision, or a professional reinventing your career with no clear endpoint in sight, this framework will help you navigate **the fog of the unknown**. By the end, you'll be equipped with a mindset and toolkit to not only achieve that elusive goal, but to grow significantly as a leader and individual in the process.

Let's begin this journey into the unknown – with open minds, steady hearts, and a spirit of adventure.

CONTENTS

1. Believe in the Unknown
2. Look Everywhere
3. Attach to the Journey, Detach from the Outcome
4. Observe, Feel, and Allow
5: The Power of Pause
6: Acceptance
7: From Analysis to Contemplation
8: Flashes of Interest
9: Pivot
10: Perseverance
11: The Contemplative Loop
12: From Control to Authority
13: Persevering Toward a Liberating Purpose

1. BELIEVE IN THE UNKNOWN

– *Trust It Exists*

Every journey into uncertainty starts with a single, radical act of trust: believing that the answer exists even if you haven't found it yet. This belief is not blind optimism; it is an intentional stance that opens you up to possibilities. High achievers often feel uncomfortable admitting "I don't know what the goal is" or "I'm not sure what I'm looking for." Yet, to achieve the unknown, you must first acknowledge its existence and value.

Embracing ambiguity begins with mindset. Allow yourself to say: *"I don't have the solution (or the end-goal) right now, but I am certain that somewhere, somehow, it is out there and will emerge."* This conviction might feel abstract, but it creates a powerful shift. By believing the unknown goal or solution exists, you prime your mind to start searching in the first place. After all, if you didn't think an answer was out there, why would you seek?

In practice, **cultivating belief in the unknown** means quieting the cynical, doubtful voice that says "What if nothing is there? What if I fail?" and amplifying the voice that says "Something meaningful is waiting to be discovered." It's a bit like a scientist believing a cure is out there before the experiments prove it, or an explorer convinced of new lands beyond the horizon. This belief fuels curiosity and courage. It also provides comfort during inevitable moments of confusion – a subtle inner knowing that *"it's okay, the answer will come in time."*

Trusting the unknown also involves a degree of humility. It's acknowledging that the universe (or the market, or your subconscious, however you frame it) holds answers or opportunities that your conscious mind can't yet grasp. Rather than forcing a premature answer, you're creating a mental space for an answer to emerge. This is a hallmark of mindful leadership: having the confidence that **not knowing is not a weakness**, but a starting point for discovery.

Reflection: Take a moment to recall a time when you faced uncertainty but later found a solution or path that you hadn't initially expected. What allowed that discovery to happen? How did your mindset or belief play a role?

Believing "it exists" is the foundation on which everything else in this framework is built. It's like planting a flag in *Terra Incognita* and saying "I will find something here." With that flag planted, you are ready for the next step: the search.

2. LOOK EVERYWHERE

– The Search with Open Eyes

Once you hold the belief that the unknown goal or answer is real, the next step is to start looking for it everywhere. When you don't know where the insight or breakthrough will come from, you must maintain a wide scope of attention. This chapter is about curiosity and openness – casting a wide net and exploring broadly, because the golden clue could be hidden in an unexpected place.

For a founder or executive used to efficiency, "looking everywhere" might sound unfocused. But searching in the context of the unknown is not aimless wandering; it's **strategic exploration**. You deliberately expose yourself to diverse ideas, people, and experiences, understanding that when the destination is unclear, **your best strategy is to increase the chances of serendipity**.

Practical ways to "look everywhere":

- **Talk to people outside your usual circle:** Seek perspectives from different industries, age groups, cultures. A casual comment from someone unrelated to your field might spark an idea or provide a missing piece to your puzzle.
- **Read and research widely:** If you're seeking an unknown solution, scan books, articles, and research papers across various domains. Allow yourself to venture down the rabbit holes of topics that interest you, even if they seem tangential – you never know what insights they might hold.
- **Observe your environment with fresh eyes:** Often the clues are around us but go unnoticed. Be present and mindful in everyday situations. You might notice a pattern in customer behavior, a passing remark by a colleague, or even an observation in nature that connects to your challenge.
- **Experiment and try small things:** Conduct mini-experiments or pilot

projects. When you aren't sure what will work, doing *something* in a low-stakes way can generate feedback. Even if an experiment "fails," it teaches you something about where the answer might or might not be.

The key is **openness** – you are essentially saying *"I'm not sure what I'm looking for, so everything is a potential hint."* This wide-open search can feel chaotic, but it's bounded by your belief and intent from Chapter 1. You're not drifting without purpose; you're **actively seeking with faith** that within the noise, a signal will appear.

During this search, it's crucial to stay **patient and receptive**. The unknown doesn't reveal itself on a convenient schedule. High-powered leaders might be tempted to set arbitrary deadlines for discovery ("I must have the strategy in two weeks!"), but often that just creates stress and tunnel vision, causing you to overlook subtle signals. Instead, maintain a relaxed alertness: **always scanning, but not in a panic**.

Remember, **"everywhere" truly means everywhere**. The breakthrough idea might come while you're listening to a customer complaint, or daydreaming on a Sunday walk, or reading a sci-fi novel at midnight. It might even come in a flash during a boring meeting when your mind wanders for a second. By looking everywhere, you ensure you won't miss it when it dances at the edge of your awareness.

Insight: Many innovative companies were born from chance encounters and cross-disciplinary insights – essentially, someone noticed something outside their main field and brought it into focus. For example, a medical advancement might arise because a doctor was curious about a piece of physics research. These breakthroughs happen because the individuals were searching "everywhere," not just in their silo.

In the journey to achieve the unknown, **exploration is your early-game strategy**. Embrace it. Enjoy it. Allow yourself to be a bit of an adventurer and a detective, combing through the world with the conviction that *the clues are out there*. This wide-ranging search sets the stage for the next fundamental shift: focusing on the journey rather than the destination.

3. ATTACH TO THE JOURNEY, DETACH FROM THE OUTCOME

A common trap when chasing goals – even unclear ones – is to become fixated on the outcome. It's ironic: we embark on an unknown quest, yet we quickly grow certain about what we think the result should be, or by when we should reach it. This chapter invites you to flip that mindset: attach yourself to the journey and detach yourself from the outcome.

Attaching to the journey means investing your energy and identity in the *process* of exploration and growth, rather than tying your self-worth (or your organization's worth) to a specific result. It's about finding commitment and even joy in the day-to-day steps: the conversations, the experiments, the learning. When you are attached to the journey, you become resilient because you measure progress in terms of experiences and insights gained, not only milestones achieved.

Detaching from the outcome does *not* mean you stop caring about success. It means you liberate yourself from the **anxiety and tunnel vision** that come with over-focusing on a particular outcome. Detachment is a paradoxical strategy: by caring less about a specific result, you often perform better and end up closer to success. Why? Because you're more present, more adaptable, and more open to unexpected opportunities. You're not derailed if things don't go as planned, because you weren't rigidly clinging to "Plan A" in the first place.

Consider a leader who is intensely attached to a preconceived outcome – for instance, launching **Product X** by **Q4** to achieve a certain market share. If evidence emerges that the market needs something different, or that the timeline is unrealistic, an outcome-attached leader might ignore those signals (after all, they're fixated on **Product X by Q4** at all costs). In contrast, a journey-focused leader remains flexible: their commitment is to *solving the customer's problem* (the journey), not necessarily to the originally imagined product or deadline. If a better solution or timeline appears, they pivot without feeling defeated – because the journey of solving the problem is still on track, even if the specifics change.

Detaching from outcomes also frees you from the fear of failure. When you're journey-oriented, a "failure" isn't a final verdict on your vision; it's just an unexpected turn in the path – sometimes a necessary one. You start to see failures as data, as part of the story, rather than as shameful mistakes. This perspective is incredibly freeing for teams as well: when a leader signals that outcomes are informative rather than punitive, the team becomes more innovative and bold.

How to practice journey-attachment and outcome-detachment:

- **Set process-oriented goals:** Instead of saying "We must reach XYZ result by January," frame a goal like "Every week we will experiment with one new idea to move closer to a solution." Make the goal about engaging in the process.
- **Celebrate effort and learning:** Acknowledge and reward the steps taken, not just the end result. If a particular approach didn't yield the big

win but taught you something valuable, that's success. Share these learnings openly.
- **Keep the outcome in view, but hold it lightly:** It's fine to have an aim or vision (you likely have some sense of what you're hoping for), but treat it as a hypothesis rather than a guarantee. Remind yourself: *"This vision is my guide star, not my shackles. I'm willing to adapt it as I learn more."*
- **Visualize the journey:** Sometimes literally mapping out the journey can help shift focus. Draw a timeline or roadmap that highlights the stages of exploration, the skills you'll build, the checkpoints of learning – rather than just a finish line. This keeps your eyes on *the road*, not just the destination.

By attaching to the journey, you also cultivate **patience**. You acknowledge that worthwhile endeavors, especially nebulous ones, take time and often don't follow a straight line. Detachment from outcome instills a sense of peace; you aren't constantly haunted by "what if it doesn't happen?" Instead, you're busy making it happen in myriad possible ways.

This journey-focused mindset sets a strong foundation. It creates a container of persistence and openness. Within that container, the next step is to fully engage with what's happening along the way – and that means heightening your powers of observation, feeling, and active participation in the present moment.

4. OBSERVE, FEEL, AND ALLOW

– The Power of Presence

On the journey into the unknown, one of your greatest allies is presence – the ability to fully experience and notice what is happening right here and now. When the final destination is unclear, the clues are often subtle and only found in the present moment. In this chapter, we delve into a triad of practices: observing, feeling, and allowing. Together, they form a way of being that keeps you connected to reality and open to insight.

Observe: Observation is about paying attention, deeply and quietly. As a leader, you might be used to taking swift action or constantly speaking; but here, you intentionally step back at times and just watch. Observe your environment, your team, your own inner state.

Notice patterns and details. In meetings, practice listening more intently – what are people really saying (or not saying)? When trying a new strategy or product, observe the results and user behaviors without immediately judging them. Become a student of the moment. The unknown often whispers before it shouts; by observing carefully, you catch those whispers.

Feel: Feeling means tuning into the emotional and intuitive signals arising within you. This can be challenging for action-oriented professionals, but it's immensely rewarding. Emotions carry information. For example, a sense of excitement about an idea might indicate a promising direction ("There's energy here, something rings true"). A feeling of dread or tightness might warn you away from a certain approach ("Something about this doesn't sit right"). Beyond emotions, bodily sensations – your **gut feelings** – can be part of this guidance system. Often, our subconscious understanding of a situation surfaces as a physical sensation or mood before our intellect catches up. By staying present to what you feel, you tap into a form of innate wisdom. **Trust what your body and heart are telling you**, even if your mind can't immediately rationalize it. Feeling also means allowing yourself to experience the frustrations and doubts that come with the unknown, rather than suppressing them. By acknowledging them, you can address them constructively.

Allow: Allowing is the art of non-resistance. It is consciously choosing not to fight or control every outcome, but to *permit* events, ideas, and emotions to unfold. This doesn't mean passive resignation; it means making space for the unexpected. **Allow things to happen without immediately trying to intervene or force them into a preconceived box.** For instance, if a new opportunity suddenly arises that wasn't in your plan, allow it a moment of consideration – could this be a path opening up? If a team member comes to you with an approach different from what you envisioned, allow the idea to breathe and be tested. When you allow, you reduce friction and anxiety. You move with the current of reality, rather than against it. This state of flow often leads to creative breakthroughs because you're working *with* the possibilities around you, not against them.

These three – observing, feeling, allowing – work in synergy. Suppose you're navigating a strategic pivot for your company in an undefined market. By observing, you might notice a faint trend in how customers are behaving. By feeling, you sense excitement when discussing one potential application of your technology, and conversely a heaviness when considering another – that's valuable data. By allowing, you let the team explore the unexpected enthusiastic option even though it wasn't part of the original plan. The combination of keen observation, inner attunement, and non-resistance often guides you toward options that the purely analytical mind might overlook.

Cultivating presence in practice:

- Start meetings or brainstorming sessions with a minute of silence or deep breathing. This may seem out of place in a corporate setting, but even a brief pause can center everyone's attention to be more observant and receptive.
- During your day, occasionally pause and take a quick mental inventory: "What am I seeing, what am I feeling, what's happening right now?" This grounds you in the present and can reveal things you'd miss on autopilot.
- When an outcome disappoints (e.g., an experiment fails, a deal falls through), observe your immediate reaction and feelings, but allow the situation to be what it is before rushing to fix it. Ask,

"What is this teaching me? What's emerging from this?" Often, a failure points to a subtle success or a next direction if you don't resist the reality of it.

- Encourage your team culture to be one of openness. For example, "open-door days" where anyone can share observations from their corner of the business. Sometimes the best insights come from unexpected sources, and a leader who is truly observing and allowing will catch them.

By mastering the art of presence through observing, feeling, and allowing, you create a fertile ground for insight. You become a sort of **antenna**, finely tuned to pick up signals from both outside (the market, the environment) and inside (your intuition, your creativity). On the journey to the unknown, *presence is a superpower*.

Now, armed with openness and presence, we encounter one of the most important milestones on this journey: acceptance. And to reach acceptance, we first talk about the power of *pausing*.

5: THE POWER OF PAUSE

– *Making Space for Insight*

In a world that glorifies hustle and rapid action, pausing can feel counterintuitive. Leaders often fear that pausing equals losing momentum. However, when your goal is unclear and the path uncertain, pausing is not a luxury – it's a necessity. Taking intentional pauses is how we create space for insight, integration, and yes, acceptance (which we will delve into in the next chapter).

What do we mean by a **pause**? A pause is a meaningful break in the frantic forward push. It's a deliberate stop where you step away from *doing* and allow yourself to *be*. This could be a five-minute breathing exercise amidst a busy day, a long walk in the middle of a workday, a weekend retreat from work to reflect, or even a moment of silence after someone asks a complex question – resisting the urge to fill the silence with an immediate answer.

Pauses serve multiple purposes on the journey of achieving the unknown:

- **Reflection:** When you pause, you give your mind a chance to process everything it has been observing and feeling. It's like hitting the "save" button on all the data you've gathered through your experiences. Often, during these reflective pauses, patterns become clear and disparate ideas connect.
- **Replenishment:** Pausing helps prevent burnout. Unknown journeys can be especially taxing because they often involve trial-and-error and emotional ups and downs. A pause is a chance to replenish your mental, emotional, and physical energy. Think of it as refueling your car during a long road trip – necessary to keep going for the long haul.
- **Perspective:** Stepping back via a pause can reveal the bigger picture. When you're mired in day-to-day complexity, a short break can help you rise above the trees to see the forest. This bird's-eye view might show you

alternative routes or confirm you're on the right path.
- **Creativity:** Neurologically, our brains often solve problems during idle times – like how great ideas famously come in the shower or on a leisurely walk. By giving yourself unstructured pause time, you invite your subconscious to play with the puzzle. Insights often bubble up when you're not actively "working" on them.

Start with small pauses and increase them over time. If you're not used to pausing, begin by inserting short breaks in your schedule. Perhaps a 5-minute pause every hour to just breathe and do nothing. Or a 10-minute quiet time mid-afternoon to sip tea and let your thoughts wander. Over time, as you see the benefits, you can make these pauses a bit longer or more frequent. For example, you might graduate to a practice of taking a half day each week away from routine tasks to reflect on the bigger picture. You might implement personal quarterly off-sites – a day or two alone or with your core team in a different environment purely to pause and contemplate direction.

Leaders often worry, *"If I pause, won't everything fall apart or slow down?"* In truth, a well-timed pause can **propel you forward**. It prevents wasted effort on false starts or misguided actions by ensuring your next step is grounded in clarity. Pausing is like sharpening the axe before cutting the tree; it feels like a delay, but it makes the work far more effective.

It's important to **encourage a culture of pause within your team or organization** as well. This doesn't mean people lounge around – it means valuing thoughtfulness. Perhaps institute a practice such as "no meeting Wednesdays" or short meditation sessions before brainstorming. When people have the mental space to think and recover, their work quality and creativity skyrocket.

To illustrate, consider a company that rushed a product to market without pausing to really integrate user feedback – they likely waste resources on a version that flops. Compare that to a company that takes an extra few weeks in a development cycle to pause after beta testing, carefully contemplate the feedback (rather than just plowing ahead with assumptions), and then pivot accordingly. The latter will produce something much more aligned with what users need. In the grand scheme, the pause saves time and leads to a better outcome.

In sum, **pausing is a skill**. You start small, build the "pause muscle," and soon it becomes a natural part of your rhythm. As you pause more, something profound starts happening: **acceptance** begins to surface. We'll explore that next, as it deserves a chapter of its own.

6: ACCEPTANCE

– The Unforced Milestone

As you practice being present and incorporate pauses into your journey, you will eventually encounter a subtle but powerful milestone: acceptance. Acceptance is a state of being where you come to peace with what is, instead of constantly fighting for what is not. It is a crucial turning point on the road to achieving the unknown, because only when you accept your current reality can you fully leverage it to move forward.

What is acceptance in this context? It's multifaceted:

- **Self-acceptance:** Acknowledging your own feelings, limitations, and talents in this journey. For example, accepting that you *do* feel afraid or uncertain, rather than masking it with bravado. Or

accepting that you need help in a certain area, rather than pretending you have it all figured out.
- **Situational acceptance:** Embracing the truth of where you are in the process. Maybe you hoped to have more answers by now, or that a certain strategy would work – acceptance means recognizing the reality (perhaps "We have not found the solution yet and that's okay, we are learning") without excess frustration or denial.
- **Acceptance of others and external factors:** Realizing that you can't control everything – the market, other people's actions, timing, etc. You stop expending energy wishing things were different and instead channel that energy into responding to things as they are.

Acceptance often **happens naturally** if you have been earnest in your journey of observation, feeling, allowing, and pausing. One day, you find that you're no longer *at war* with the unknown. The anxious question "Why haven't I figured this out yet?" fades. You understand at a gut level that *this is a process* and you're genuinely okay with that. It's as if you've reached a scenic overlook on a hike – you're not at the summit yet, but you can pause, catch your breath, and appreciate how far you've come and the view of the valley below.

It's important to note: **you cannot force acceptance**. Just as you can't yank a plant out of the ground and stretch it to make it grow faster, you can't *make* yourself or your team fully accept a situation before you naturally arrive at that point. Acceptance requires time and processing. That's why the previous chapter on pausing is so essential – those pauses give your psyche the room to process and arrive at acceptance in its own time.

When acceptance hits, it often comes with a feeling of relief and clarity. For instance, you might realize and truly accept that the original product idea you had isn't viable. There's no more denial or bargaining; you see it clearly and you're at peace with moving on. Or you accept that a certain beloved team member, while wonderful, is not the right fit for the next phase of the project. Instead of avoiding the truth, you face it calmly. This acceptance then **unlocks progress** – because now you can take action based on reality, not on wishful thinking.

Cultivating acceptance:

- **Acknowledge small truths regularly:** Don't sweep inconvenient truths under the rug. In team discussions, make it a practice to say things like "Let's be honest with ourselves about what these numbers imply" or "I sense that we are struggling to admit X – what would happen if we did?" By normalizing honest acknowledgement, you pave the way for collective acceptance.
- **Embrace vulnerability:** As a leader, if you demonstrate acceptance of your own vulnerabilities ("I'm not sure about this and I'm okay admitting that"), you set a tone that it's safe for others to do the same. Shared acceptance grows in such safe spaces.
- **Mindful practices:** Techniques such as mindfulness meditation can indirectly foster acceptance. By regularly sitting with whatever thoughts and feelings arise, you train your mind to not resist reality. Over time, this carries over into your work and leadership: you become more able to sit with an uncomfortable truth without denying it.

- **Frame challenges as reality checks, not failures:** When something doesn't go as hoped, instead of reacting with "This is a failure, unacceptable!", try "This is what's happening; let's accept it so we can learn from it." This shifts the focus from judgment to understanding.

Acceptance is a milestone, not an endpoint. Reaching acceptance doesn't mean you have "solved" the unknown goal yet. It means you have reached a calmer, clearer mental state from which you can continue your journey more effectively. In the timeline of this framework, acceptance often marks the end of the initial exploratory phase (where things might have felt quite turbulent internally) and the beginning of a more focused, creative phase. It's like the moment when a caterpillar becomes a chrysalis – not yet a butterfly, but having undergone an important internal transformation that will *allow* the next stage to happen.

Having found acceptance, you are now ready to deepen your exploration through a more deliberate practice: contemplation. In the next chapter, we'll differentiate **contemplation from**

mere analysis, and see how it propels you forward once you've accepted where you are.

7: FROM ANALYSIS TO CONTEMPLATION

– Deepening Your Understanding

After acceptance, you may find yourself in a calmer space where you can truly think and feel deeply about your challenge. This is where we shift from basic analysis to the richer practice of contemplation. Both analysis and contemplation are valuable, but they are not the same.

Analysis is something most professionals are well-trained in. It involves breaking a problem into parts, examining data, identifying patterns, and coming to logical conclusions. Analysis is largely a rational, left-brained activity. For example, analyzing your business might involve reviewing metrics, segmenting your customers, calculating ROI, etc. It's about understanding "what happened" and "what is happening" in a structured way.

However, **analysis alone has limits** when dealing with the unknown or something novel. By definition, analysis deals with what is known (data points, past events, present observations). It might tell you that a marketing strategy isn't working or that a certain demographic is responding better to your product – useful information, but it won't automatically spark the *new* idea or reveal the *hidden* solution. That's where **contemplation** comes in.

Contemplation is a broader, more holistic form of thinking. It's not just a mental exercise; it engages intuition, imagination, and subconscious processing. When you contemplate, you are essentially **sitting with a question or concept in a relaxed, open state of mind**, allowing insights to arise rather than forcing a conclusion. If analysis is like methodically decoding a puzzle, contemplation is like observing the puzzle pieces quietly until a big-picture image suddenly "clicks" in your mind.

Think of analysis as a subset of contemplation: you might begin by analyzing aspects of your situation to gather facts (that's the structured part), and then you step back and *hold all those facts together softly in your mind*, watching how they interrelate, and feeling which pieces resonate or not. In contemplation, you give equal respect to logical thoughts and to **intuitive hunches** or emotional responses that come up about those facts.

How to practice contemplation:

- **Create a contemplative setting:** This could be during one of your extended pauses – perhaps in a quiet room, or in nature, or late at night when the world is silent. Be comfortable and free of distractions. Have a journal nearby to jot down thoughts, but start by just sitting with your thoughts.
- **Focus on an open-ended question:** Instead of asking a binary or a very specific question ("Should we launch Product A or B?"), pose something open like "What is trying to emerge here?" or "What does our customer truly need that we haven't seen yet?" or even "What feels most alive in our business right now?". Let your mind explore freely.
- **Use visualization or daydreaming:** Imagine various scenarios, without the pressure to immediately decide. Let

your mind wander into "what if" territory. What if we completely re-imagined our strategy? What if I were in the customer's shoes? What if this obstacle is actually an opportunity in disguise? Allow scenarios to play out in your mind's eye.

- **Pay attention to feelings and body responses during contemplation:** This ties back to Chapter 4. As you entertain different ideas or insights in contemplation, notice how you feel. Sometimes a new possibility will bring a sense of excitement or relief – a sign it may be on the right track (even if it's scary or unconventional). Conversely, a thought might bring a tightness or dread, indicating a path that maybe isn't right, or a fear you need to understand.
- **Be patient and gentle:** Contemplation isn't about arriving at an answer in one sitting. It's more like steeping tea – the flavor (insight) deepens the longer you let it be. You might spend several sessions over days or weeks contemplating aspects of your unknown quest. Little by little, clarity

emerges. It may come as a gradual understanding or occasionally as a sudden "aha" moment.

It's worth highlighting the difference between **productive contemplation and unproductive rumination**. Contemplation is **curious, open, and exploratory**. Rumination, on the other hand, is when your wheels are stuck spinning on the same anxious thought loop ("Why can't I figure this out? I'm stuck. This is hopeless…"). If you find yourself ruminating, that's a sign to step back – perhaps return to a pause or do something to break the cycle (take a walk, talk to a friend, etc.). Contemplation should feel like it expands possibilities or understanding, whereas rumination feels like it narrows and stresses you.

One practical technique is **journaling** during or after contemplation. Write down the insights or questions that arose. Sometimes writing helps clarify fuzzy thoughts. Over a period of contemplation, you can review your journal and notice emerging themes or answers.

Another technique is **dialogue** – talking out loud either to yourself, a confidant, or even to an empty chair (some leaders talk to an imaginary version of their customer or mentor). The act of verbalizing thoughts without the pressure of immediate feedback can surface insights. It's akin to brainstorming, but in a gentle, introspective way.

From filtering to focusing: As you contemplate, you are effectively **filtering information and ideas**. Earlier, during analysis, you might have gathered a lot of data – some useful, some noise. In contemplation, the unimportant details often fade away ("peripherals" get discarded) and the core signals shine through. By allowing your mind to sift things in an unforced manner, you'll naturally begin to focus on what truly matters. It's like panning for gold – your contemplative mind swirls the pan, and the gold nuggets (key insights) start to separate from the silt.

By the end of a good contemplative phase, you'll likely have a clearer sense of direction. You might not have a full blueprint, but you might realize "This aspect is key; I should pursue it further," or "These ideas I've been considering don't actually matter – I can let them go." In essence, contemplation bridges the gap between **where you are (accepted reality)** and **where you could go (envisioned possibilities)** by providing depth of understanding.

Armed with the fruits of contemplation, you will start noticing sparks – the "flashes of interest" that hint at something worth exploring. In the next chapter, we'll discuss recognizing these flashes and taking action on them, which moves us into the realm of pivoting and persevering.

8: FLASHES OF INTEREST

– *Recognizing and Following the Sparks*

One beautiful outcome of deep contemplation (and the whole process up to now) is the appearance of flashes of interest. These are those sudden sparks in your mind – a surge of curiosity, an exciting idea, a pattern that suddenly makes sense, or a gut feeling pointing you in a new direction. They often appear as subtle glimmers at first, but they carry a disproportionate significance. This chapter is about noticing those flashes and having the courage to follow them.

Think of flashes of interest as your intuition and intellect collaborating to say, *"Pay attention to this!"* It might be a random thought that crosses your mind in the shower, a line from a book that resonates deeply, a suggestion from a team member that grabs your attention, or a new metric that suddenly stands out. After all the filtering and pausing, your mind is primed to notice these things – but you must remain receptive.

Recognizing a flash of interest:

- It often comes with a quick jolt of energy. For example, you're reading a market research report and one insight makes you sit up straighter, thinking "There's something here."
- It may initially be accompanied by uncertainty or fear ("This idea is intriguing but it sounds crazy!"). That's okay – don't dismiss it just because it's unconventional. Often, the unknown thing we're seeking lies outside our comfort zone.
- It sticks around. Unlike fleeting random thoughts, a true flash of interest tends to linger in your mind, inviting you again and again to consider it. If you find yourself returning to an idea repeatedly with curiosity (even if it's inconvenient or not fully logical), that's a sign.
- It feels meaningful. You might not fully understand why, but it feels like a piece

of a puzzle that clicks, or at least *could* click if further explored.

Once you recognize such a spark, the next step is crucial: **explore it**. This is the point where you shift from contemplation (internal reflection) to **experimentation or action** on that specific insight. You don't have to commit your entire life or company to it yet; you're just giving it a chance to show you more.

How to follow a flash of interest:

- **Research or gather more information:** If your spark is a concept or technology you know little about, do a quick deep dive. See what's out there, who else is doing it, how it might solve your problem. Keep your research focused and don't get lost in analysis paralysis – you're just trying to illuminate the idea a bit more.
- **Prototype or test on a small scale:** If the spark is an idea for a new product feature, service, or strategy, create a small experiment around it. For instance, if it's a new feature idea, can you mock it up or test demand with a subset of customers? If it's a new strategy, can you run a short pilot

program? The goal is to get real-world feedback.
- **Discuss it with others:** Sometimes voicing the idea to a trusted colleague, mentor, or friend can clarify it. Their reactions and questions will help you refine your thinking. Be selective – choose someone open-minded who understands the spirit of your exploration. You're not looking for immediate validation or invalidation, just perspective.
- **Journal or map it out:** Write down the idea in detail. Sketch how it might work or how you might pursue it. Externalizing it on paper can transform a nebulous spark into a more structured plan.

Crucially, **don't ignore the spark**. In the grind of professional life, it's easy to push aside a new idea because it feels inconvenient or risky. Many people have moments of inspiration that they never act on – only to see someone else later succeed with a similar idea and think, "I thought of that!" The difference often is simply **action**. By exploring your flashes of interest, you give them a chance to grow from a spark into a flame.

This doesn't mean every spark will turn into a roaring fire of success. Some will fizzle out – perhaps the idea isn't feasible, or the interest fades after deeper investigation. That's fine. The purpose of following sparks is twofold: you either discover a promising path (great!), or you learn that particular spark was a dead-end which still teaches you something (also useful!). In both cases, you're better off than ignoring it.

Sometimes, following one spark leads to another. You start exploring an idea and in the process discover an even more intriguing question or a problem that *actually* needs solving. This is the nature of the unknown journey – it can zigzag. The spark you follow might not be the final answer, but it may illuminate the next step of the path.

By cultivating attentiveness to these flashes and a habit of pursuing them, you essentially keep the **momentum of discovery** alive. Your journey remains dynamic and responsive to what you're learning.

Now, as you act on these flashes of interest, you will inevitably find yourself needing to make larger adjustments – to change course in meaningful ways based on what you discover. This leads us to the concept of **pivoting**, which we will explore in the next chapter. Pivoting is the skill that ensures your journey remains aligned with the freshest insights and realities, rather than clinging to old plans. It's a critical ability on the road to achieving the unknown.

9: PIVOT

– Embracing Change on the Journey

In startup language, a pivot is when you change direction with your product or business strategy based on what you've learned. In our broader context of achieving an unknown goal, pivoting means adjusting your path when new insights (from those flashes of interest, experiments, or changing circumstances) indicate that a different approach would be wiser. Pivoting is not a sign of failure; it's a sign of growth and responsiveness. It's how you stay aligned with reality and opportunity.

By the time you reach this stage, you have: believed in your unknown goal, searched widely, detached from rigid outcomes, practiced presence (observe-feel-allow), made space through pauses, gained acceptance, contemplated deeply, and followed sparks of interest. This journey so far has likely revealed a clearer picture of what the true goal or solution might be, or at least what it is not. Armed with that knowledge, a pivot could be gentle or dramatic: maybe a slight course correction or a complete re-imagining of the project.

Why pivoting is powerful: It acknowledges that **the path to success is rarely straight**. Especially when dealing with uncharted territory, you seldom get everything right on the first try. Pivoting allows you to integrate what you've learned and start anew from a more informed position. It's like sailing – you might have to tack (zigzag) as the winds change, but each tack moves you closer to the destination given the wind's reality.

Emotional aspect of pivoting: Pivoting can be emotionally challenging. It often involves letting go of something that you initially built or believed. You might worry about sunk costs – "But we've already invested so much in this direction!" Or you might fear how it will look to others – "Will people think I'm inconsistent or lost?" This is where your earlier cultivation of detachment and acceptance pays off. If you've truly detached from a specific outcome and accepted reality, you'll see pivoting for what it is:

not a personal or moral failing, but a smart and necessary progression.

How to pivot effectively:

1. **Recognize the signs:** Common signals that a pivot is needed include persistent lack of progress, feedback indicating a misalignment (e.g., customers don't get value from your offering), internal team misgivings that grow over time, or the emergence of new opportunities that render your current approach less attractive. Thanks to your observant and contemplative mindset, you'll likely sense these signs earlier than most.
2. **Revisit your vision:** Take a step back and remind yourself of the core vision or purpose behind your journey. A pivot should always serve that deeper purpose, even if the method of achieving it changes. Ask, "What are we really trying to accomplish at the end of the day, and does our current approach do it? If not, what might?"
3. **Generate alternatives:** Brainstorm possible pivots. This could mean targeting a different customer segment, applying your solution in a different

industry, using a different technology, changing your business model, or redefining what "success" looks like. At this stage, think broad – multiple options for how you could change course.

4. **Evaluate and decide:** Use both your analytical and intuitive skills to assess the alternatives. Which option resonates most with the knowledge and gut feelings you've accumulated? Which feels like it addresses the core problem or leverages your core strengths better? There might not be a single perfect option, but there will likely be one or two that clearly stand above the rest in viability and alignment with your vision.

5. **Communicate and execute:** If you're leading a team, communicate the pivot clearly and honestly. Share *why* you're pivoting – frame it in terms of learning and adapting to better achieve the mission. This helps others buy in and not view it as a haphazard whim. Then, make a plan for executing the change: reassign resources, set new goals or metrics, and so on. Essentially, treat

the pivot as a new mini-journey – with its own kickoff.

6. **Carry lessons forward, leave baggage behind:** Importantly, take with you the lessons and assets from your previous efforts that still apply, and consciously drop the rest. Pivoting often fails when people try to drag along all their old assumptions and processes into a new direction. Be willing to start fresh where needed. You're not starting from scratch (you have experience now), but you are starting anew.

One more thing: **once you've learned the skill of pivoting, it stays with you**. You become less afraid of change. You start to see change as a constant companion rather than an enemy. In fact, you might pivot not just when something isn't working, but even when something *is* working, if you see a way to make it dramatically better. That's the mindset of innovation – never get too comfortable with "good enough," always be open to a pivot that could lead to greatness.

Pivoting also has a cumulative effect. Each pivot is like a loop in a spiral taking you closer to your ultimate goal. You try, you learn, you pivot –

each cycle reveals new insights and gets you a bit closer (even if indirectly) to achieving the unknown outcome you seek. This iterative, non-linear progress is what we'll explore in the next chapter, tying together the ideas of perseverance and the looping journey toward your goal.

10: PERSEVERANCE

– Fuel for the Long Haul

Pivoting is critical, but knowing when and how to pivot doesn't replace the need for perseverance. If pivots are course corrections, perseverance is the engine that keeps you moving no matter how many turns the road takes. It is the steadfastness, the will to continue, that carries you through the iterative loops of trial, insight, and adjustment.

Achieving something truly novel or unclear is rarely a quick win. It tests endurance. There will be moments – even after a well-executed pivot – when progress is slow, doubt creeps back in, or external obstacles appear. Perseverance is what keeps you going through these moments. It's a deep resolve that **"I will see this through"**.

It's worth reflecting on the nature of perseverance. It is not stubbornness or blind persistence on a fixed idea (remember, we've let go of rigid attachment to any single outcome or plan). Instead, perseverance is a commitment to your *purpose*, to the journey itself, and to the faith that your continued efforts will pay off. You can pivot 100 times if needed, but you *persevere* in the overarching quest.

Building and maintaining perseverance:

- **Connect with your purpose regularly:** Remind yourself *why* you embarked on this journey in the first place. Is it to solve a meaningful problem for people? To achieve a personal dream that won't let go of you? To create something that hasn't been seen before? Keeping that purpose front and center stokes the fire of perseverance. Some people keep a written mission statement or a vision board visible in their workspace for this reason.
- **Celebrate small wins:** Perseverance is strengthened by acknowledging progress, no matter how small. Did you solve a minor technical issue? Gain a new insight? Get positive feedback

from one user? Each of those is a victory. In the long journey, these are your fuel stops. Take time to appreciate them and even celebrate with your team – it builds morale and reminds everyone that *movement is happening.*
- **Maintain your well-being:** It might sound mundane, but basic self-care is foundational to perseverance. It's hard to persist if you're running on empty physically or emotionally. Ensure you get enough rest, maintain some exercise routine, and have support systems (friends, family, mentors) to talk to. Burnout is the enemy of perseverance, so watch for its signs and address them proactively (sometimes that means taking a **pause** again to recharge!).
- **Develop resilience to criticism and setbacks:** Not everyone will understand your journey into the unknown. Some may criticize or doubt you. Setbacks, as we discussed, are inevitable. Perseverance means cultivating a mindset where criticism is taken as feedback (if useful) or brushed off (if not constructive), and

setbacks are seen as learning steps. This is where not taking things personally (as mentioned in earlier chapters) really helps – it prevents emotional exhaustion from external negativity.
- **Flexible persistence:** The marriage of pivoting and perseverance is **flexible persistence**. You persist in the mission, but you flex in the method. You don't give up on the goal, but you are willing to adapt how you get there. This kind of persistence is intelligent and dynamic, not brute force on a dead-end.

It's also helpful to recall inspiring examples when thinking of perseverance. History and business lore are full of stories where perseverance made the difference. Thomas Edison famously said about inventing the lightbulb, "I have not failed. I've just found 10,000 ways that won't work." He kept going until one did. In the modern startup world, entrepreneurs pivot their companies multiple times and often face near-death moments, but those who eventually succeed are the ones who **refused to quit** – *and* kept learning and adapting as they pushed forward.

For you as a mindful leader, perseverance might sometimes mean **standing up for your vision when it's unpopular**, or continuing to invest in an R&D project that hasn't borne fruit yet because your gut says it's promising, or simply showing up each day with renewed commitment even when results haven't materialized yet. It can be quiet and dogged or it can be bold and outspoken, depending on the situation – but it is always about not giving up the core quest.

Now, perseverance doesn't mean never, ever giving up on a *specific* idea. We've already embraced that certain approaches will be let go (that's pivoting). But perseverance is about not giving up on *the pursuit of a solution*. It's saying, "I will keep finding a way, if not this way, then another."

Let's also be honest: persevering through unknown territory is **hard**. There will be days of frustration, maybe even despair. It's in those times that the earlier elements of this framework bolster you: your belief that an answer exists, your connection to purpose, your acceptance of reality, your ability to pause and recuperate, and your willingness to adapt. All of these are like scaffolding supporting your perseverance.

With strong perseverance, you continue through the iterative cycles needed to reach your goal. And this leads us to a crucial insight: the path to achieving the unknown is not linear, but **circular or spiral** – you will find yourself looping through phases of pausing, contemplating, pivoting, and pushing forward multiple times. This iterative loop is how progress is born from the unknown. In the next chapter, we'll put it all together and examine this **contemplative loop** that ultimately gets you to your destination.

11: THE CONTEMPLATIVE LOOP

– Iteration Toward Progress

By now, you've gathered all the key elements of the framework: belief, exploration, detachment from outcome, presence, pause, acceptance, contemplation, sparks of interest, pivot, and perseverance. These do not simply occur in a straight line, one after the other, never to be seen again. Rather, you will cycle through them repeatedly in various combinations – each cycle bringing you closer to the ultimate goal or revealing a refined version of it. This is the contemplative loop: an iterative process of learning and evolving, driven by reflection and action.

Let's visualize this. Imagine a looping pathway, like a spiral that circles upward. Each loop consists of phases of **contemplation** (pausing, reflecting, generating insights) followed by **pivoting/persevering** (making changes, taking action, and pushing forward). With each loop, you're not simply covering the same ground; you're rising to a higher level of understanding and closeness to the goal. You revisit similar questions or challenges, but with new knowledge and perspective each time.

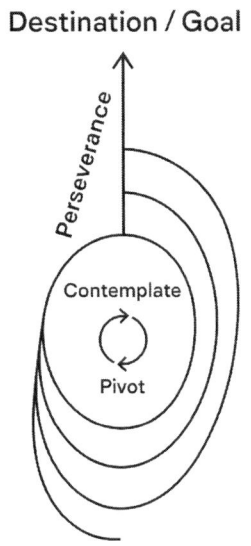

In the figure above, notice how **perseverance is depicted as the fuel that keeps the loops going** (an upward momentum), and **pivoting (guided by contemplation) is what changes**

the direction of each loop slightly, aiming it closer to the "destination/goal." The goal sits at the top not as a fixed point you shoot straight for, but as something you approach via this circling route. The journey is not a ladder; it's a spiral staircase.

Why a loop and not a line? Because, as we've established, the unknown is rarely conquered by a single plan executed flawlessly from point A to point B. It requires adaptability (hence, loops) and depth (hence, contemplation). Each loop can be thought of as one "chapter" or phase of your project or quest: - In one loop, you might be focused on understanding the problem deeply (lots of research and contemplation, culminating in a decision to pivot your approach to the problem). - In the next loop, you're building a prototype or implementing changes (action and perseverance, culminating in new feedback from the world). - In the next loop, you pause to contemplate that feedback (what worked, what didn't, what's the market telling you now?), which leads to another adjustment or pivot. - And so on.

This continues until one day, you break through – you achieve what was once unknown. Perhaps you realize you've developed the innovative product that fulfills the need, or you've found the career that was your calling, or your organization has discovered a novel strategy that sets it apart. Interestingly, when you reach the "top" of one spiral (goal achieved), you often see new horizons – the next unknown challenge or a refinement of the original goal emerges, and a new spiral begins at a higher level. That's why truly growth-oriented leaders see their journey as never really ending, just evolving.

Making the loop work for you: - Be **conscious of which phase** you're in. Ask yourself: Am I in a contemplative phase right now (seeking insight, pausing, analyzing, ideating)? Or am I in an execution phase (testing, doing, building, persevering)? Both are necessary, and knowing where you are helps you apply the right mindset. Sometimes individuals or teams get stuck in one phase – e.g., endless contemplation without action, or frantic action without reflection. The magic lies in the balance and alternation. - **Transition deliberately** between phases. When you've acted and gathered data, make a deliberate shift to contemplative mode (perhaps scheduled as a review meeting or personal reflection day). Conversely, when insight strikes and a plan forms, consciously move into action mode (set goals, assign tasks, move!). Mark the transitions so that you and your team know, "Alright, we've thought, now let's do," or "We've done a lot, now let's think." - **Document learnings each loop.** Keep a log of what you learn every cycle. It might be as simple as a "lessons learned" doc or a quick presentation to your team. Over time, this documentation becomes a treasure trove of wisdom. It also helps onboard new team members into the journey, showing them how you got here. - **Stay open to surprise until the end.** One loop might very late in the game reveal something dramatic. (For instance, you're almost ready to launch, and a beta tester's feedback uncovers a feature that turns out to be the true linchpin of your product's success.) Be willing to incorporate even last-minute insights; don't fall into the trap of, "We've iterated enough, now we stick blindly to plan." The framework is about trusting that iterative process until *and even after* the goal is met.

The contemplative loop is essentially the embodiment of *wisdom in action*. It's how mindful leadership operates in practice – always learning, always adapting, yet always moving forward with purpose. It's iterative, but not aimless; flexible, but not without direction.

At this point, our framework's core is complete. However, before we conclude, it's important to address how this internal journey of achieving the unknown reflects in your outward leadership. In the final chapter, we'll discuss how all of this transforms you as a leader – particularly how it helps you move from a paradigm of control to one of true authority, and how it aligns you with a purpose that is not only successful, but liberating.

12: FROM CONTROL TO AUTHORITY

– The Mindful Leadership Mindset

Embarking on the journey to achieve an unknown goal doesn't just get you to a destination – it changes you along the way. Perhaps one of the most profound shifts is how you lead and how you relate to control. Traditional management tactics emphasize control: setting exact targets, strict plans, tight oversight of others. But as you've seen, rigid control is antithetical to navigating the unknown. In fact, the very process we've discussed – believing without seeing, detaching from outcomes, allowing things to unfold, iterating through uncertainty – has likely made you a different kind of leader by the end: one who leads with authentic authority rather than mere control.

Let's clarify the terms: - **Control** in a leadership context is about exerting power, often through micromanaging, imposing one's will, and trying to guarantee outcomes through force or strictness. It comes from a place of fear – fear of failure, fear of chaos, fear of looking bad. When we operate from control, we often stifle creativity and demoralize teams, and ironically we can miss great outcomes because we're fixated on a narrow plan. - **Authority**, on the other hand, is a more natural, earned influence. It's the kind of leadership that people trust and willingly follow. Authority is built on expertise, integrity, empathy, and the capacity to inspire. A leader with authority doesn't need to control every detail, because they've set a clear vision, built a strong culture, and empowered others – thus things tend to organize and align without coercion. Authority comes from a place of confidence and service, rather than fear.

Through the journey we outlined: - When you **admit you don't have all the answers** and start seeking, you demonstrate humility. Paradoxically, this increases your authority in the eyes of others, because you're being real and showing that you value learning over ego. -

By **attaching to the journey and detaching from outcomes**, you model resilience and level-headedness. Your team sees that you are committed yet not panicked; this earns respect. You're not throwing blame when things go wrong (a habit of a control-based leader), but instead calmly course-correcting, which reinforces a stable environment. - Your practice of **observing, feeling, and allowing** makes you a more empathetic and perceptive leader. You listen to others; you notice concerns; you create space for innovation. People feel heard and seen by you. That psychological safety boosts their performance and loyalty. Instead of controlling them, you're empowering them – and they respond by stepping up, which in turn validates your leadership. - **Pausing and acceptance** show that you are a thoughtful leader, not a reactive one. You aren't making knee-jerk decisions to assert control. Instead, you pause to gather wisdom and you accept truths even when they're inconvenient. This integrity and composure give you a gravitas – people start to say, "Our leader doesn't rush to judgment; they consider things carefully," which increases their trust in you. - Through **contemplation**, you likely come up with more innovative and well-rounded solutions than you would by brute analytical force alone. When your team or stakeholders see those insights – especially when you credit the process and collective input rather than claiming personal genius – your authority grows. You're seen as a visionary, yet also as someone who leads collaboratively. - When you follow **flashes of interest and pivot boldly but wisely**, you demonstrate courage and adaptability. Instead of clinging to control and doubling down on a failing plan (to "save face" or out of stubbornness), you show the confidence to change course for the greater good. That authenticity (doing what's right over what's easy) makes people respect you deeply. It shows you prioritize the mission over your ego. - Your **perseverance** shows commitment. A controlling leader might demand perseverance from others while themselves panicking or switching priorities haphazardly when things get tough. A mindful authoritative leader, by contrast, exemplifies perseverance. You're there in the trenches with your team, day after day, optimistic and steady. That inspires others to persevere too. They trust that "we'll get there because our leader won't give up, and won't let us give up either, even as we adapt."

In sum, by transforming how you approach the unknown, you have also transformed how you wield power. You've moved from a stance of *controlling every variable* to *guiding with vision and trust*. This transformation is exactly what was meant by "turning control into authority." You now have the authority that comes from authenticity, insight, and integrity, rather than the shallow authority (in name or position only) someone might try to enforce through control.

This shift has practical benefits: - You can delegate more effectively. Because you're not micromanaging and you trust the process (and your people), you give team members autonomy. This often leads to better results as people take true ownership of their work. - You respond to crises or changes with more agility. A control mindset might freeze or shatter when plans fall apart; an authority mindset observes, accepts, pivots and inspires others to follow suit. - Your leadership style becomes a model that others in your organization adopt. An organization filled with empowered, reflective individuals who aren't waiting for top-down orders can achieve far more in uncertain environments than one where everyone's waiting for permission and fearing punishment.

Lastly, it's worth noting the personal dimension: letting go of control in favor of mindful authority tends to make you, the leader, **happier and more fulfilled**. Control is exhausting. It pits you against reality – an unwinnable war. Authority, conversely, feels natural; it's about harnessing reality. You're working with the flow of your team's talents, with the flow of the market's signals, and with your own inner wisdom. This alignment reduces stress and increases a sense of purpose.

Speaking of purpose – throughout this journey there has been an undercurrent of something greater: the notion that what you're striving for is not just any goal, but a *liberating purpose*. In the final chapter, let's reflect on how pursuing an unknown with this mindful, persevering approach can lead you to a purpose that is truly transformative – not just for external success, but for your own evolution and freedom.

13: PERSEVERING TOWARD A LIBERATING PURPOSE

There's a phrase that has echoed in this book: "liberating purpose." It points to a purpose or goal that, in the pursuit or achievement of it, also liberates you (and perhaps others) in some way. But what does that really mean, and how does our framework help you find or fulfill such a purpose?

A **liberating purpose** is one that aligns deeply with who you are and brings out your highest potential. It's "liberating" because working toward it frees you from the trivial, the false, and the limiting aspects of life. It has a quality of **service and inspiration**. Often, it's a purpose that not only accomplishes something externally significant (like building a great company or solving a big problem) but also transforms you internally. It feels like stepping into your own

authority (as discussed in the previous chapter) and living with authenticity and impact.

Many people have goals, but not all goals are liberating. Some goals can even feel like prisons – e.g., pursuing something just because society expects it, or chasing a number (money, followers, etc.) that ultimately feels hollow. A liberating purpose, in contrast, feels deeply meaningful; it energizes you and others. It "liberates" by unleashing creativity, passion, and a sense of connection to something bigger.

The journey to achieve an unknown as laid out in this book is almost tailor-made to help you discover or fulfill a liberating purpose:

- **Starting with the unknown:** If your true purpose was obvious and on the surface, you'd already be doing it. Often, our liberating purpose lies hidden behind layers of fear, social conditioning, or simply unawareness. By setting out believing in an unknown, you give yourself permission to seek something *truly yours*, not just the next logical step on a generic success path.
- **Following flashes of interest:** Those sparks you learned to follow? They are often breadcrumbs to your purpose.

Our deepest gifts and callings leave clues in what fascinates us, what problems deeply bother us, and what ideas won't leave us alone. By honing in on those and exploring them, you may stumble into a mission that you didn't initially set out to find, but that was waiting for you.

- **Pivoting when needed:** Sometimes you start with a purpose that you think is "it," but as you grow, you realize it was a stepping stone to something even more resonant. Being willing to pivot means you don't get stuck on an old idea of who you are or what you should do. You let your purpose evolve as you do. For example, maybe you started a company to solve Problem X, but through the journey you discovered the real issue you're passionate about is Problem Y, so you steer the company towards Y. That's a purpose pivot, aligning closer to what truly matters.
- **Perseverance and integrity:** A liberating purpose will often test you. It's usually not the easiest path (at least not at first) – if it were, everyone

would do it. There may be sacrifices or doubters. Your perseverance, coupled with the mindful practices of this framework, ensures you keep going *and* keep growing through those tests. Each cycle of challenge and reflection deepens your commitment and clarity.

- **Mindful leadership and authority:** As you transform into a leader who values trust over control, you are actually creating the conditions to live out a great purpose. Why? Because big purposes typically require rallying others, inspiring stakeholders, maybe even birthing a movement. By becoming the kind of leader who leads with wisdom and heart, you attract support and build communities around your purpose. People want to be part of what you're doing, because they see the genuine passion and care. In turn, that community can amplify the impact of the purpose, making it even more liberating for a wider circle.

It's also worth noting that sometimes the **journey itself** *is* the liberating purpose. That is, the reason you felt called to chase an unclear goal might be because the process would shape you into someone new. We often think of purpose as a single external mission ("My purpose is to accomplish X in the world"), but equally, your purpose could be to evolve into a certain kind of person or to master a certain quality. For instance, perhaps your deeper purpose is to achieve personal freedom and wisdom, and the mechanism life gave you was this challenging project or leadership role. By going through it mindfully, you unlock that personal liberation – regardless of the external outcome.

However, more often than not, internal and external purposes converge: by growing internally, you achieve something externally that is meaningful, and vice versa. That synergy is the sweet spot of a liberating purpose.

Signs you are aligning with a liberating purpose:

- You feel more alive and "on-track" even if the work is hard. There's a sense of *rightness* about what you're doing.
- The work (or journey) calls forth your best qualities – courage, compassion, creativity, resilience – and you find yourself rising to the occasion.

- Others resonate with the value of what you're pursuing. They might say things like, "It's inspiring to see you do this," or "We really need this in the world." A liberating purpose tends to have a ripple effect, liberating or uplifting others too.
- Fear and doubt don't disappear, but they no longer govern you. You notice that even when you're afraid or unsure, you have a deeper trust (in yourself, in the process, in the meaning of the work) that carries you through.
- Success metrics might change for you. While you still care about concrete results (profit, growth, etc., if it's a business context), you also start to define success in terms of fulfillment, impact, and authenticity. You could look back and say, "Even if this hadn't succeeded on paper, I would still be glad I pursued it because of who I've become and what I've learned."

To tie everything together: **persevering toward a liberating purpose** means you keep going not just to "win" in the conventional sense, but to fully realize the meaningful vision that has emerged for you. By doing so, you not only reach a goal – you *liberate* a new level of potential in yourself and perhaps in others. It's the ultimate win-win: achievement coupled with personal transformation.

As we conclude, remember that this framework is a guide, not a dictate. Your journey will have its unique twists and turns. Embrace them. Use this framework as a compass rather than a map – it will help you orient yourself in the dark forests of the unknown, but it won't dictate every step (nor should it; half the beauty is discovering your own path).

In the final words, let's recap the essence of this journey and send you off with encouragement for the road ahead.

Embracing The Journey, Empowered For The Unknown

We set out to create "a framework for achieving anything unknown," and along the way, we discovered it's as much about who you become as it is about what you achieve. The path through uncertainty – believing, exploring, detaching, observing, pausing, accepting, contemplating, pivoting, persevering – transforms you into a more mindful, resilient, and authentic leader. It equips you with the inner authority to handle whatever comes next, known or unknown.

To summarize the journey:

1. **Believe in the unknown:** Trust that the answer or vision exists, even if you can't see it yet.
2. **Look everywhere:** Stay curious and open; search in unlikely places and welcome diverse inputs.

3. **Attach to the journey, detach from the outcome:** Commit fully to the process and experience, but release the obsession with specific results. Paradoxically, this leads to better outcomes.
4. **Observe, feel, allow:** Practice presence. Notice the details, heed your intuition, and let events unfold without constant interference.
5. **Pause and accept:** Take regular pauses to reflect and recharge. Allow acceptance to naturally arise – of yourself, the situation, and others – creating a foundation of reality from which to build.
6. **Contemplate deeply:** Go beyond surface analysis. Spend time in thoughtful reflection to filter what matters and invite fresh insights.
7. **Catch the sparks:** Pay attention to flashes of interest and emerging ideas. Explore them; they are often keys to innovation.
8. **Pivot gracefully:** When new information or insights indicate a better path, be willing to change course. Adaptation is strength, not weakness.

9. **Persevere with purpose:** Keep going with determination and flexibility. Fuel your journey with the conviction of your mission and the lessons you've learned.
10. **Iterate upward:** Recognize that progress will come in cycles, not a straight line. Each loop of reflection and action takes you higher and closer.
11. **Lead with authority, not control:** Trust the process, trust your team, and trust yourself. Lead by example, with clarity and empathy, instead of clinging to control. This earns true respect and loyalty.
12. **Find liberation in purpose:** Aim for a goal that not only succeeds in the market or field but also resonates deeply with your values and growth. Let the pursuit of it set you free and inspire others.

Remember that no journey is without difficulties. There will be times when you feel lost, times when the unknown feels too unknown. In those moments, return to the basics: take a pause, breathe, maybe even flip back to a chapter of this book that calls to you. The answers might not be immediate, but they will come – often just when you're about to give up, a light appears.

Also, know that you are not truly alone on this path. Many have walked it or are walking it – every trailblazing entrepreneur, every transformational leader, every creative genius faces the blank canvas of uncertainty and must conjure something from nothing. They too have battled doubt and fear. What sets those who succeed apart is rarely just raw talent or luck; it's the mindset and persistence we've discussed. It's the willingness to venture into the unknown and make it an ally rather than an enemy.

As you close this book and continue on your quest, carry with you a sense of **adventure and trust**. The unknown, in truth, is not empty – it's full of possibilities. By believing in it, you invite those possibilities into your life. By journeying with mindfulness and courage, you turn those possibilities into reality.

In the end, achieving the unknown might surprise you. You may find that the goal you reach is different from the one you initially thought you wanted – and yet exactly what you needed. You may discover that the greatest reward is not the treasure at the end, but the person you became and the lives you touched along the way.

Here's to your journey into the unknown – may it be filled with growth, discovery, and the fulfillment of a purpose that truly liberates the best in you and those around you.

Thank you for reading. Now, the next steps are yours to take.

Other Books By Ramit Soni

It Takes a Village to Raise a Leader [Abridged Version] - A reflective summarized guide to community, leadership, and personal growth.

It Takes a Village to Raise a Leader [Full Version] - Stay tuned for the author's next release

Made in United States
Cleveland, OH
10 September 2025